Copyright © 2016 Nutrition Associates, LLC

All rights reserved. No part of this book may be reproduced, transmitted, or stored in an information retrieval system in any form or by any means, graphic, electronic, or mechanical, including photography, taping, and recording, without prior written permission from the author.

Second US edition 2016

ISBN-13: 978-0692651940 (Roni Roth Beshears)

ISNB-10: 0692651942

Illustrations were done by Rob Peters in pen, ink, and 6B pencil on Bristol paper and digitally painted in Photoshop.

All matters regarding weight management and health require medical supervision. The author is not engaged in rendering professional advice or services to children and their families or caregivers. The ideas, procedures, and suggestions contained in this book are not intended as substitutes for consulting with your medical-care provider. All matters regarding schools and their policies on bullying should be directed to appropriate school personnel. The author shall not be liable or responsible for any loss or damage allegedly arising from information or suggestions in this book. The author does not assume any responsibility for errors or for changes that occur after publication. The author does not have any control over and does not assume any responsibility for author or third-party websites or their content.

To contact Dr. Roni Roth Beshears and to schedule a book and program presentation, please email her at roni.nutritionassociates@gmail.com.

For Children
Who Have Experienced
Weight-Based Name-Calling
—RRB

Foreword

Please Don't Call Me Chubby Roni! is a story about the harm of name-calling in the school setting for a young girl who is overweight. The actions taken by the main character, Roni, and her teacher raise awareness about weight-based bullying in the classroom. The book serves to open communication with children, parents, and teachers about negative body-size talk and the impact it can have on children. Questions for discussion are included for children, teachers, and parents.

The Roni Children's Book Series is an educational and engaging teaching tool for school-age children and their families. The series supports the establishment of nonthreatening and wholesome environments to help children grow, learn, and accomplish their dreams.

Other books in the series are *Roni Takes Action* and *Roni Goes to Camp*.

Places for book distribution are homes, libraries, schools, community centers, and medical practices.

Thanks to Adrienne Forman, MS, RDN, a child weight-management specialist with the MEND (www.healthyweightpartnership.org) program, for suggesting the book's title *Please Don't Call Me Chubby Roni!* and providing valuable resources and comments.

School pictures were scheduled for tomorrow.

"I want to look really good," I whispered to myself while standing in front of my bedroom closet.

"Wow, this dress is perfect," I said with delight.

Taking the dress out of the closet, I arranged my outfit on a chair for school the next morning.

"Mom," I said while eating breakfast, "I want to look awesome for my class picture today. Will you help me with my hair?"

Most of the time, my hair was a mess in the morning. I was always in a rush to get to school on time. This day was special.

At school, the class was escorted to the auditorium for pictures.

When it was my turn, the photographer positioned me on a stool against a large blue-and-white school banner.

"Ravioliiiii," he shouted to get my attention. I sat perfectly still with a big smile on my face.

One by one, all the students had their picture taken.

As I watched, I said to Jackie, "Some kids are short, and some are tall. We come in many shapes and sizes. Don't we?"

"Just like a box of animal crackers," Jackie replied.

We both laughed.

For the group picture, we were placed in line according to height. I felt awkward being one of the tallest in class.

Sarah, another tall girl, said to me, "Roni, don't feel bad. Kids grow and develop at different rates."

"How do you know?" I said.

"My mom's a doctor," Sarah told me.

"Yeah," I said to her, "that's why we all come in different shapes and sizes."

The photographer started shuffling us around on the stage platform for the class picture.

"I don't like being in the middle of the group," I told a short boy named Max, standing next to me.

"Taller kids are usually placed in the back," I explained to Max.

"One day I'll tower over you, Roni," Max predicted.

A few weeks later, I found a large envelope with the class photo on my desk.

I opened it slowly.

To my surprise, Sam, the boy at the desk next to mine, yelled, "Hey, **Chubby Roni,** is that you in the middle?"

The kids laughed and my face turned bright red.

I'd never been called **chubby** before, and it hurt!

I ran home from school, opened the front door, threw my backpack on the floor, went to my room, and slammed the door shut.

"Roni," Nana said while knocking on my door. "How was your day at school? Why did you run up to your room without saying hello?"

I didn't answer. She knocked again.

"Roni, are you all right?"

I opened the door and said, "Hi, Nana."

"You're upset, Roni. What happened? How was your day at school?"

"Not good," I replied.

She looked concerned. "Let's go downstairs and talk about your day."

"Do you want to tell me what happened at school today?"

She went to pick up my backpack. I said quietly, "Nana, look inside."

"Roni, why is your picture scratched out?"

I took the photograph from her and said, "Sam, a boy in class, made fun of my picture and called me **chubby**."

Nana was speechless.

At the kitchen table, Nana said, "Roni, it hurts when a classmate is mean. You don't deserve to be spoken to that way by a student or by anyone."

She looked me straight in the face and said, "Roni, I understand how you feel. I'm sure you will know what to do."

Later that evening, I was busy doing homework when Dad entered my room.

"Roni, you're upset," he said. "Hurtful comments about appearance are unacceptable. Would you like me to speak with the boy, his parents, and your teacher?"

I just sat at my desk, numb.

Mom entered the room.

"Roni, often kids are picked on for looking different."

She lowered her voice and said caringly, "No matter what shape or size a person is, it's important to accept oneself and take steps to be healthy, like we do as a family."

Before leaving my room, she turned to me and said, "You are my pride and joy. Remember, we are always here to help."

I tossed and turned the whole night in bed.

"What am I going to do?" I kept repeating to myself. "I can't let Sam get away with calling me **chubby**."

"Kids my age grow at different rates, as my friend Sarah told me. I'm not going to feel bad about myself."

"I must have courage," I thought.

When I entered the classroom the next day, I was scared. Sam might say something else hurtful to me and embarrass me in front of the class.

I took a deep breath and walked up to Sam and said, **"Please Don't Call Me Chubby Roni!"**

He looked surprised, as if he'd forgotten what he said to me the other day.

I repeated, **"Please Don't Call Me Chubby Roni!"**

Walking back to my desk, Rosa, my best friend, and a few girls gathered around me to offer support.

Ms. Chen, our teacher, stopped by my desk, having overheard my remark to Sam.

"Sit down, girls," she said. "Go back to your desks. Class is starting."

Ms. Chen stood in front of the class, as she usually did, but this morning was different.

"Words are powerful," she said in a no-nonsense way. "Name-calling is not tolerated in my class."

Ms. Chen went to the board and started listing words.

She asked the class, "Who can tell me why I wrote these words on the board?"

"Max, go ahead. Tell us," Ms. Chen said.

"The words relate to body size."

"Go on," she insisted.

"The words in the first column are similar to one another, and so are the words in the second column. But the first- and second-column words are opposites."

Max said in a soft voice, "Calling someone fat or skinny is unkind."

Ms. Chen then asked, "Do these words describe how healthy we are?"

The whole class said, "NO."

Ms. Chen pointed to the board and said, "These words are hurtful. Let's remember to be kind to each other."

Chubby Scrawny

Fat Small

Heavy Skinny

Husky Slim

Plump Thin

As Ms. Chen arranged our desks in four groups, she said, "Your assignment today is to develop wellness recommendations. The four categories are food, fitness, feelings, and friends."

"After lunch, each group will share their recommendations with the class," Ms. Chen instructed us.

At lunch, Sam came over to me.

"Roni, I'm sorry for calling you **chubby.** At home, my dad calls my sister **chubby,** and I didn't think it was bad."

I said, "Sam, it's not OK for anyone to use words like that—not you, your dad, or anyone."

Back in class, the kids assigned to the "food" group came up with a list of healthy recommendations:

* Eat fruits and vegetables often.
* Enjoy breakfast every morning.
* Limit sugary drinks, cake, candy, chips, and cookies.
* Drink plenty of water daily.
* Choose reasonable portions, not supersized portions.
* Make good food choices at fast-food places.

The "fitness" group shared their list next:

* Participate in daily exercise, like bicycling, dancing, walking, or any physical activity you like to do.
* Limit time watching TV and playing computer or video games.
* Get enough sleep.
* Practice safety, like wearing bike helmets.
* Have fun being active.

The "feelings" group had recommendations:
* Know your strengths and weaknesses.
* Feel good about yourself.
* Ask for help if someone makes you feel bad.
* Think positive thoughts.
* Smile often.

The "friends" group had a few suggestions:

* Stay away from mean kids. Let them know it's not OK to be hurtful to another.

* Talk to a best friend or family member if you have a concern.

* Seek out understanding adults at school, like a school counselor or favorite teacher.

* Be your best self.

After class that day, I breathed a sigh of relief, knowing that Ms. Chen would not tolerate name-calling in class.

Nana was right. I was able to figure out how to handle a bad situation with the support of my family, friends, and teacher.

I repeated to myself my motto, "Doing is freeing. Free to be the best that I can be."

Afterword

Children deserve the support of caring adults, family members, and teachers to combat the harm that can result from weight-based name-calling and bullying, whether at home, at school, in the neighborhood, or online.

It is important to recognize weight-based bullying to prevent children from feeling alone and powerless. Effective strategies in school and at home are necessary to protect children who are ostracized and stigmatized due to body weight.

This book was written to help parents, caregivers, and teachers navigate this sensitive subject with children.

All children should strive to be healthy, have a positive body image, and feel good at any size. There's no better gift we can give a child.

Questions for Discussion

For children who are overweight, to recognize weight-based name-calling

Have you ever been called hurtful names or teased because of your weight?

How did it make you feel?

Who was responsible for hurting you?

Has this person called you names before?

Did your friends or classmates stick up for you?

Have you told your parents, grandparents, teachers, or school counselors about these negative comments?

For all children, to raise awareness about weight-based name-calling

Is it OK to call someone fat, fatso, fatty, or similar words?

How would you feel if someone said a hurtful comment about your appearance?

Would you stand up and support a child who is teased about body weight?

Do you think male or female models in fashion magazines represent how all of us should look?

Do professional sport players all look alike? Who do you admire?

Are you aware that we all come in many shapes and sizes and that we come from different families, cultural backgrounds, and traditions? Could it be that each one of us is special and unique?

How can we be sensitive to all children and promote kindness, no matter what shape or size others may be?

For teachers, to address weight-based name-calling at school

Are you alert for weight-based name-calling in the classroom, in the lunchroom, in the school hallway, or on the playground?

Have you shared your concerns with students and parents?

Is there a support system in place at school to help children who have been victimized due to body weight?

What classroom strategies can be implemented to embrace a no-tolerance policy for weight-based name-calling?

For parents of children who are overweight, to increase awareness about the possible consequences of weight-based bullying

Have you noticed uncommon signs or behavior by your child that may signal a problem at school or elsewhere?

Ask your child the following questions: Have you been made fun of, called names, or teased at school? Is your classroom teacher supportive of you? What about other teachers?

Ask yourself what you can do to help your child. If necessary, request a referral to a mental-health professional skilled in this area from the school counselor or your child's medical provider.

Recommended Online Resources

New York Times
 www.well.blogs.nytimes.com/2015/07/07/
 fat-stigma-fuels-weight-bullying/

Obesity Action Coalition
 www.obesityaction.org/understanding-obesity-
 in-children/childhood-obesity-stigma

United States (U.S.) Department
of Health & Human Services
 www.stopbullying.gov

University of Connecticut Rudd Center
for Food Policy and Obesity
 www.uconnruddcenter.org/weight-bias-stigma

WebMD
 www.webmd.com/parenting/raising-fit-kids/
 weight/talk-obesity-bullying

About the Author

As an advanced-level nutrition practitioner, **Dr. Roni Roth Beshears** has worked at the local, state, and federal levels with food and nutrition programs and services. As a community volunteer and advocate, she has devoted time and energy to serving the needs of vulnerable women, children and families. Dr. Roth Beshears is a registered dietitian nutritionist and certified health and wellness coach. She is a graduate of Syracuse University (BS) and Columbia University, Teachers College (EdD).

www.ingramcontent.com/pod-product-compliance
Lightning Source LLC
LaVergne TN
LVHW071028070426
835507LV00002B/74